ALL I NEED TO KNOW I LEARNED FROM MY COLLEGE BAR

ALL I NEED TO KNOW I LEARNED FROM MY COLLEGE BAR

Written by Adam Lorenzo

Illustrated by Antonio Pinna

Cover design & Illustrations by Antonio Pinna

Edited by David Bushman
Book designed by Adam Lorenzo

Published in the USA by Fayetteville Mafia Press
Columbus, Ohio

Contact Information
Email: fayettevillemafiapress@gmail.com
Website: fayettevillemafiapress.com
Twitter: @FMPBooks
Instagram: @Fayettevillemafiapress

ISBN: 9781949024562
eBook ISBN: 9781949024579

Dedicated to my dad … Paul Lorenzo.

Without his help, none of this would have been possible.

PREREQUISITE

The only prerequisite for this education is that you know how to read. So if you just read that ... congratulations! You have been accepted.

But before you unpack and get settled, do your due diligence and ask your parents if they paid, aka "bribed," anyone for you to get admitted into college.

Ask if they falsified any documents, like your SAT scores, or used Photoshop to prove that you're on the crew team, even though you have aquaphobia, get motion sickness, and hate sports. We know that's your face, but is that really your athletic physique in a crew uniform?

This is important. So, off the record, I wouldn't even say it's a bad idea to take a peek at your parents' checkbook. Do you see any checks in the amount of, oh, let's say $1.2 million? Are the checks made out to the college you attend or your college's crew coach or his charity? If so, that's a red flag. If not ... great news! The flag is green!

INTRODUCTION

Hello! Hello!

This is a true story. Mine. I owned a cathedral of knowledge known as a college bar . . . while I was in college at Syracuse University.

I'd write my papers at the bar, sneak out of class to get beer deliveries, tend bar every night, and at 3:00 a.m. I'd climb in the dumpster and jump on the garbage bags to get the lid closed . . . so the waste company would empty it. Then I'd be at class at eight the next morning.

I spent many nights sleeping on the floor in the bar's "office" (janitor's closet) and I loved every zzzz . . .

Because it was the kind of college bar that's cherished universally: sticky floors, a Wall of Fame, a Wall of Shame, it served green beer and Lucky Charms on Saint Patrick's Day, the walls were covered in hypnotic beer neons, there was a pool table, dart machine, and people would write their names on dollar bills and stick them to the wall.

Then at closing time, people would try to steal the neons, pool cues, darts, and dollars on the wall or anything that wasn't bolted down . . . tight (garnish trays, shot glasses, doors to the bathroom stalls).

A college bar is a rite of passage, a home away from home, full of people who are every size/shape/color and same economic status . . . broke.

It's where you meet new friends, hook up (for an hour, one night, or forever), and celebrate all the major holidays . . . Mardi Gras, Halloween, Game Day, Pledge Week, and every Thursday-Sunday.

But most importantly, a college bar is where you'll have the best time of your life . . . before becoming respectable tax-paying citizens (shockingly).

There's a reason Elon Musk said, "Don't confuse schooling with education."

Because life experiences = wisdom. And I learned more invaluable life lessons in that business than in any classroom.

And that's what this humor/life-wisdom book is about—thinking, not drinking.

It's also why I think at the end of your college career, you should be able to honestly say to yourself:

"If I would've spent all of the time I spent in this college bar actually studying, I'd be a doctor."

If you can say that, you made the right choice.

Case in point . . . soon after graduating, I applied the knowledge I had learned in my college bar to change career paths and achieve my dream of becoming a comedy TV/movie writer in Hollywood.

And one of the first things I learned when I owned that college bar was the importance of bonding with people. So let me tell you how I got here:

I got my first staff-writing job by sending jokes to David Letterman. No joke. His company, Worldwide Pants, called me on a Friday with "good news" and "bad news."

The "good news" was they offered to put me on the writing staff of *The Late Late Show with Craig Kilborn* (a dream come true)! What could be "bad news"?

They said, "You need to let us know your answer by 5 p.m. and move to Los Angeles by Sunday (forty-eight hours later) so you can start on Monday."

Now that doesn't sound bad, but I had just gotten engaged, she didn't want to move to LA (I don't blame her; her family lived in NY), and we had our engagement party that same Sunday. Gulp.

I'd never been to LA, didn't have a car, and my new home was a small motel across from CBS Studios.

I started out a superstitious writer, so I thought I had to write everything on my "lucky" desktop computer, which I had sent to the motel. When I arrived, I found the box and everything in it . . . soaking wet and smashed to smithereens.

It was like the FedEx guy hit the box with a sledgehammer or a humongous cartoon mallet and then ran it over to make sure it was dead.

Luckily . . . in a college bar, anything that can go wrong does go wrong. So I was an expert at jumping over impossibly high hurdles.

And the next morning I started work on *The Late Late Show*. The first two celebrities I remember seeing are Salma Hayek and George Clooney!

My office was in a trailer on the roof, next to a helipad. College bars prepare you for performing on practically no sleep. So I'd regularly be the first person to arrive in the morning.

I'd often see a helicopter descend out of the orange-pink sky, land, and Dan Rather would hop out holding a cup of coffee.

I'd step outside, he'd salute me, I'd salute back, and then he'd disappear into a secret door to talk to the president of the United States or maybe he'd just go to work, reporting news. And I'd go write jokes about the same stories.

I stayed writing for late-night TV for a while . . . a college bar also supplies you with a lot of fodder for funny! I sold jokes to Jimmy Kimmel, Martin Short, and Tina Fey/Jimmy Fallon on *Saturday Night Live*'s "Weekend Update."

I was then advised to start writing sitcoms. Going from writing jokes to writing sitcom/movie scripts is a totally different craft . . . not an easy transition.

So I had to apply the most valuable lesson I had learned in my college bar . . . Hustle! Hustle! Hustle! And then all of the muscles of life that I developed in that college bar—started paying off!

My TV/movie writing credits include:

Emmy-winning *Everybody Loves Raymond*, *Are We There Yet?* (starring Terry Crews and Ice Cube), and *Everybody Hates Chris*, created by the wildly talented Ali LeRoi and Chris Rock.

I've written for Oscar-winner Mel Gibson, David Kohan and Max Mutchnick (creators of *Will & Grace*), Paramount, Warner Bros., Sony, NBC/Universal, Disney, Mattel, MTV Studios, and DreamWorks.

And I'm just getting started! (I got that first staff-writing job when I was only twenty-six.) Still no joke! Which brings me to my first book . . .

All I Need to Know I Learned from My College Bar

So here's your first lesson: if you have a dream, no matter what it is, go for it! Because if I can do it, you can do it too! As long as you buy and read this book. Otherwise, you literally have zero chance.

I want to leave you with this cool statistic that I just read:

The University of al-Qarawiyyin is considered the most ancient university in the world still operating. It was founded . . . in 859 AD.

And the first college bar was founded . . . 1 day later.*
*Probably.

Cheers!
Adam Lorenzo

Are you feeling overwhelmed?

Don't worry! There's a solution . . .

GO TO A COLLEGE BAR!

Sure, use the credit card your parents gave you in case of an emergency. Tell them I said it was okay.

If they don't believe you, they can call me:

323-403-7864

Never put your real phone number in a book.

First, finish your homework!

Do the things in life that you <u>don't</u> want to do **FIRST**, so you have more time to do the things you want to do.

Success = opportunity + preparation.

SO ... BE PREPARED!

What to bring to a college bar checklist:

- Aforementioned credit card.
- Contraception.
- ID proving that you're 21. (Wink.)

Remember the Three Ds.

Unlike the three Rs that are the basic skills taught in schools: <u>R</u>eading, <u>W</u>riting, and <u>A</u>rithmetic. Three Rs? Huh? The three Ds actually make sense:

1.) <u>D</u>on't do drugs.
2.) <u>D</u>on't have unprotected sex.
3.) <u>D</u>on't drink and drive.

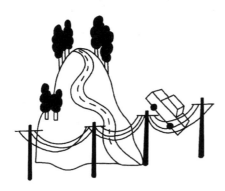

Here's a bonus fourth D:

4) <u>D</u>o what you love
and the money will follow.

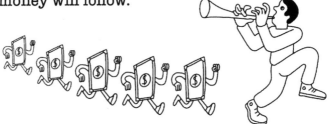

Sit up front!

It's impossible to be unhappy during Happy Hour!

Sometimes you just need a drink.

Sometimes you need a fishbowl.

You get what you pay for.

So order the good stuff!

Remember, if your problem can be solved with money ... you *don't* have a problem.

Be generous ... tip well!

If you're not making mistakes, you're not trying hard enough.

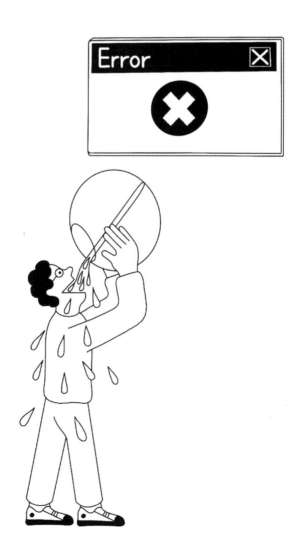

**And if you don't learn from your mistakes ...
why bother making them in the first place?**

LESSON LEARNED

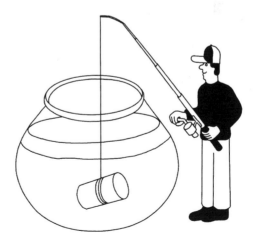

LESSON LEARNED

Your cell phone is for answering, not checking.

Turn off your phone, your brain, and watch TV for an hour.

Breathe. It calms the nervous system.

Breathe in through your nose for ten seconds ...

Hold the breath in for ten seconds ...

Blow it out of your mouth for ten seconds.

Order a hamburger!

Wait. Make it a cheeseburger!

Get the fries!

Stick out your hand, introduce yourself, and make a new friend!

Extra tip: Compliment their name.

For fun, stick out your hand, introduce yourself, and make a new friend ... in Chinese!

For more fun, stick out your hand ... introduce yourself as someone that you're not ... and make a new friend! Go ahead!

Choose your friends wisely.

Studies show how successful you will become is determined by the people you spend the most time with.

Friends also increase longevity ...

unless your friends are murderers.

Look people in the eyes ...

Only if they're talking to you.

Otherwise, looking into someone's eyes is creepy.

Listen more than you talk.

It's why you have two ears and one mouth. *

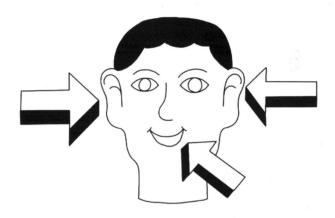

*Not applicable if you only have one ear, like the praying mantis.

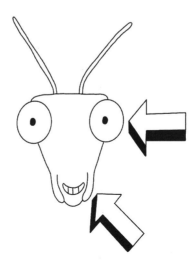

Every meeting is a possible opportunity.

People will tell you everything you need to know about them in the first fifteen minutes of meeting them.

14 minutes later ...

Don't interrupt people when they talk.

Don't use four-letter words.

Go where the love is.

If someone doesn't want to be your friend, go find another friend.

Four-letter-word them.

Laugh.

Play games.

Participate in a turtle race!

Slow 'n' steady wins the race.

Winners always stick their neck out.

You'll never know what you're capable of unless you try.

Finish strong!

But let other people win sometimes too.

Studies prove your brain releases endorphins when you win.

So let people think they feel awesome because they're hanging out with you ... not the "winning" chemicals.

And don't gamble!

The only way to win at gambling is ... not to bet.

Listen to music ... and sing!

In a college bar!

In the shower!

In the car!

And stop picking your nose in there. We can all see you. WTF?

Dance! Dance! Dance!

It's okay to look silly ... just be you!

Types of Dances

Raise the Roof

Snoopy/Peanuts Dance

Break-Dance

The Robot

The Chicken Dance!

*Tap!

* This could get you punched.

Don't fight!

Forgive quickly.

You can't do wrong by doing right.

Don't sweat the small stuff. Stress kills.

The best things in life are free ...

But 2-4-1 is still a pretty good deal.

Enjoy the little things

... Every drink!

... Every sandwich!

... Every pee!

When peeing: Spell your name, spell the name of your favorite sports team, or pretend you're putting out a barn fire.

Pursue your dreams!

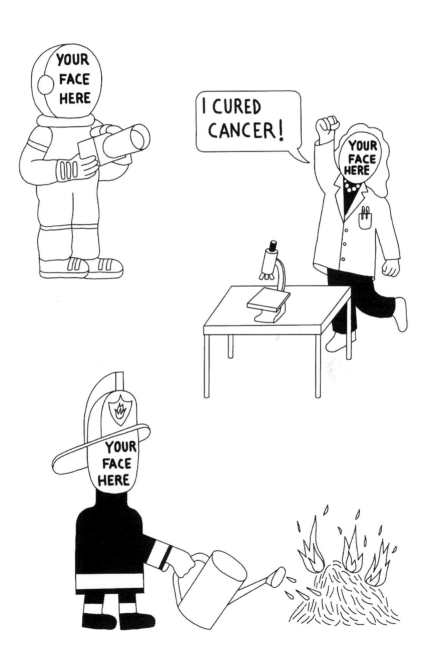

Sometimes you have to believe in yourself before anyone else does!

Those who dare ... win!

Don't settle!

Ask out the person you're really attracted to.

The worst anyone can say is "No."

"No" is just a word. *

* Unless they say "Helllllll No!"

Say YES!

See! At any second ... something great can happen to you.

Have faith (in something bigger than you).

The difference between a wish and a dream ... is an action.

10 YEARS LATER

If you're gonna do something inevitably, do it immediately!

Time is your most valuable asset.

Do everything in moderation.

Be the best part of someone's day or you're wasting your life.

Anonymously:

- Take a roll of quarters and put them in expired parking meters.
- Shovel your elderly neighbor's driveway.
- Call your parents and tell them that you love them.
- Put someone else's shopping cart back.
- Bring someone (professor, dean, or bartender) an apple pie.
- Leave a $20 bill in a park playground, in a church, or send it to me and I'll consider putting it in a park playground for you.

My address is:
9190 W. Olympic Boulevard #109
Beverly Hills, CA 90212

Never put your real address in a book.

Be a great kisser.

Be direct.

Say *Please.*

And *Thank You.*

Get your daily supply of Vitamin N!

Vitamin N = Nature

Wish on the first star you see!

Star light, star bright,
First star I see tonight,
I wish I may, I wish I might,
Have this wish I wish tonight...

Sample wishes:

... Please let my roommate not be home.

... Please let me get an erection even though I'm drunk.

... Please let there be a condom in my purse.

... Please let him get an erection even though he's drunk.

... Peace on Earth.

Be in awe.

There's gotta be aliens!

Use your imagination.

Try new things!

Don't be selfish.

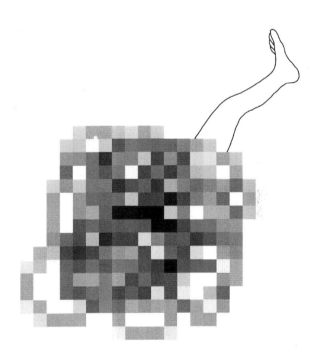

Take directions.

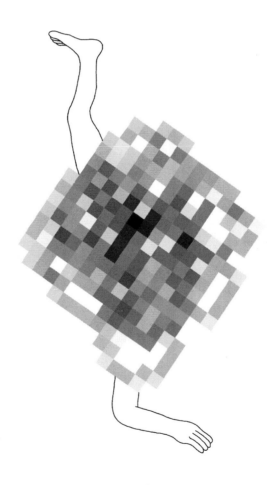

Practice good hygiene.

Get a good night's sleep.

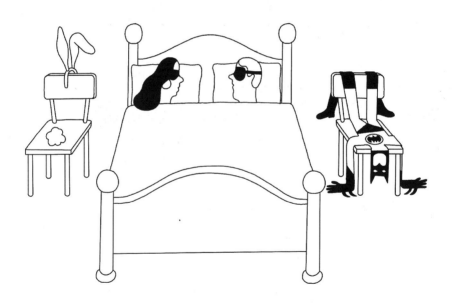

Either you set your day up or your day will set you up.

Recipe For Starting Each Day Off Right!

- Get on your knees and Thank God (or your Higher Power or Aliens) for another day on the right side of the grass.
- Say "Good morning" to the person next to you in bed ... even if you don't know their name. Just say, "Good morning ... you!"
- Eat a healthy breakfast.

**Suit up and show up ... on time
(even if you're hungover).**

Warning: Drinking too much coffee makes you anxious. If you really need a pick-me-up, eat an apple, it does a better job. No joke.

Pay attention and work hard!

You gotta have the bad days to know the good days.

Sometimes you'll think you're having a bad day and you're not. Remember if you're depressed ... feelings aren't facts.

THINGS THAT INCREASE SEROTONIN AND MAKE YOU FEEL BETTER:

1) EXERCISE.

2) LISTEN TO LOUD MUSIC.

3) EAT DARK CHOCOLATE.

4) GET SUNSHINE.

Let's be serious for a moment. Zzzzz. But seriously, it takes courage to get help, so if you need help, here's the number for the National Suicide Prevention Hotline:

800-273-8255

It's hardest when you're the closest to reaching your goal.

It's not how many times you get knocked down that counts.

It's how many times you get back up!

Everything you want is on the other side of fear.

Never quit before the miracle!

Live your best life!

And once you achieve your dreams ... remember that you have to give your gifts away in order to keep them.

When we get, we make a living.
When we give, we make a life.

And if you ever start feeling overwhelmed ...

Don't worry! There's a solution

GO TO A COLLEGE BAR!

This College Diploma belongs to

_____

Proudly sign your name here

This Degree Of

BACHELOR OF SMARTS

WITH ALL THE RIGHTS AND PRIVILEGES THEREUNTO
APPERTAINING.

APPROVED BY:

Adam Lorenzo
CHANCELLOR

Adam Lorenzo
PRESIDENT

Adam Lorenzo
CHAIRPERSON

ABOUT THE AUTHOR

Adam Lorenzo started as a joke writer, selling material to Tina Fey and Jimmy Fallon on *Saturday Night Live*'s "Weekend Update"; Jimmy Kimmel; and David Letterman, which resulted in his first staff-writing job, on *The Late Late Show with Craig Kilborn* (cocreated and executive produced by Letterman). Other TV credits include the Emmy-winning *Everybody Loves Raymond*, *Are We There Yet?* (starring Terry Crews and Ice Cube), and *Everybody Hates Chris*, based on the life of Chris Rock. Lorenzo grew up in Buffalo, New York, and now lives in Los Angeles, writing for hit television comedies.

ABOUT THE ILLUSTRATOR

Antonio Giovanni Pinna is an award-winning freelance illustrator based in Milan, Italy.

His work has been featured in the Society of Illustrators, American Illustration and Communication Arts Illustration Annual. With a worldwide client list that includes *Penguin*, the *New York Times*, and the *New Yorker*.

He finds his inspiration in old illustrated books, movies, and nature.

Antonio's graphic style and conceptual approach to illustration result in a refreshingly simple yet original illustration. He combines his unique sensibility with humor to arrive at truly novel design solutions.

ACKNOWLEDGMENTS/ SPECIAL THANKS

I would like to truly thank everyone I ever talked to, or served a drink to, in that college bar. It's not realistic to think that I can remember all of your names. But you know who you are. And I'm still gonna try! So here it goes. Thank you:

All employees of Maggie's, Lefty, Ali, Mace, Ella Lupo, Antontio Pinna, Paula, Judit, Scott, David, Kevin Garlitz, Jeff Haskett, Ann, Coco, Noelle, Billy, Al, Kimberly, Scully, Elon, Funny Guy in the Red Shirt, Funny Guy in the Red Shirt's Girlfriend, Girl Who Always Brought in Her Dog, Coco, Paisley, Ian, Ian's Mom, Dad and Brother, Flip-Flop Phil, Michelle, Professor LaHood, Dan, Bobby King, Jo-Jo, Charlie, Julie, Gina, Frank, Tommy, Raj, Dancing Woman in the White Jeans, Drunk Santa, Joel W. in Alex Bay, the Mayor, Mrs. Mayor, T-Bone, Craiggers, Jerry, Captain Morgan and His Morganettes, D.J. Bill B., Guy Who Taught Me How to Make a Kamikaze, Rick, Mike, Mel, Trace, Micky, Jackson, Irwin, Keith, Tony, Kelly—the guy Kelly—the girl, Michael, Electra, Axil, Tina, Laurie, Florence, Ria, the Fishbowl Salesman, Gavin, Couple with the Cool Boat, Jet Ski Guy #1, Jet Ski Guy #2, Jet Ski Guy #3, Vin, Aaron, Lucy, Howard, Topless Girl and her boyfriend Topless Guy, Chicken Dance Guy, Wynona, Keanu, Customer Who Left Me a

$100 Tip, Person Who Left Their Golf Clubs at the Bar—I
still have them if you want them—Ronny, Harry, Bruce,
Bucky, Deli, the Guy Who Always Parked Illegally, Majiid,
Shawn, Jimmy, the Fort Drum Military Base, pretty
much the entire population of Canada, Fisherman Sam,
Massimo, Woodrow, every member of every fraternity and
sorority in the world, college sports fans, college football
teams, college basketball teams, college baseball teams,
college volleyball teams, Senator—you know who I'm
talkin' about! John, Ken, Andrew, Frank, Manny, Larry,
Ed, Robert, Chris, Dee, Mitch, Buck, Kate, H. Howser,
Scott, Mr. Binger, Barefoot Guy, Coach Josephs, Sergeant
A., Ginger, all the bachelor parties, all the bachelorette
parties, all the AC/heat repairmen, Peanut Shell Pete, Clay,
DT, David Letterman, the Blessed Mother Mary, Saint
Jude, Saint Joseph, Sister Virginia, Sister Mary Bernard,
and most of all . . . thank you!

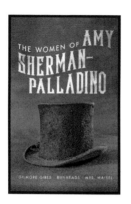
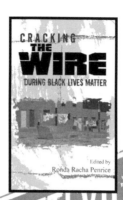

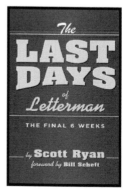